Ankita Rossi

Donau Radweg
(Danube River Cycle Path)

Title: Donau Radweg (Danube River Cycle Path)
Author: Ankita Rossi
Published by: NEXTUNICORN PUBLISHER PROPRIETORSHIP
Publisher's Address: Shree Dwarkadhish Ji Ka Was, Emri, Rajsamand, RAJASTHAN, India. Pincode: 313342
Printer Details: Published online on various platforms.
Edition: 01
ISBN: 978-81-968464-6-6

Images Source: Pixbay: (https://pixabay.com/)
All images' rights belong to their respective owners.
Disclaimer: The author and publisher disclaim all liability for accuracy, loss, or damage arising from the use of this travel guide; users are urged to independently verify information and prioritize personal safety.

Catalog

Welcome to the Donau Radweg Experience 1
   Scenic Serenity 3
   Danubian Delights 4
Donau Radweg's 19 Must-Visit Destinations 5
   1. Passau, Germany: 5
   2. Regensburg, Germany: 6
   3. Kelheim, Germany: 7
   4. Ingolstadt, Germany: 7
   5. Eichstätt, Germany: 8
   6. Straubing, Germany: 9
   7. Deggendorf, Germany: 10
   8. Schlogen, Austria: 11
   9. Linz, Austria: 12
   10. Grein, Austria: 13
   11. Melk, Austria: 14
   12. Dürnstein, Austria: 15
   13. Krems, Austria: 16
   14. Vienna, Austria: 17
   15. Bratislava, Slovakia: 18
   16. Gabcikovo Dam, Slovakia: 19
   17. Komárno, Slovakia: 19
   18. Budapest, Hungary: 20
   19. Danube Bend, Hungary: 21
Need to Know for Donau Radweg Adventure 23
Itineraries 25
   Danube Cycling Odyssey - 2 Weeks 25
   Danube Delta Discovery 26
Danube Cycling Retreat - Accommodation Guide 28
1. Riverfront Inns and Guesthouses: 28
2. Traditional Austrian Mountain Huts: 28
3. Urban Retreats in Linz: 28
4. Quaint B&Bs in Wachau Valley: 28
5. Danube Delta Riverside Cabins: 28
6. Historic Pensions in Bratislava: 29
7. Budapest Boutique Hotels: 29
8. Cyclist-Friendly Hostels: 29
9. Lakeside Campgrounds near Linz: 29
10. Quirky Convents along the Danube: 29
Visas and Residency Along the Danube Cycling Route 30
Seasonal Highlights Along the Danube Cycling Route 32
Danube Radweg Detailed Route Descriptions 34
1. Passau, Germany, to Regensburg, Germany: 34
2. Regensburg, Germany to Kelheim, Germany: 34
3. Kelheim, Germany to Ingolstadt, Germany: 34
4. Ingolstadt, Germany to Eichstätt, Germany: 34
5. Eichstätt, Germany to Straubing, Germany: 35
6. Straubing, Germany to Deggendorf, Germany: 35
7. Deggendorf, Germany to Schlogen, Austria: 35
8. Schlogen, Austria to Linz, Austria: 35

9. Linz, Austria, to Grein, Austria: 35

10. Grein, Austria, to Melk, Austria: 36

11. Melk, Austria, to Dürnstein, Austria: 36

12. Dürnstein, Austria, to Krems,Austria: 36

13. Krems,Austria, to Vienna, Austria: 36

Key Junctions on the Donau Radweg 37

List of 2 Hotels in Each Key Junctions 40

1. Hotel Weisser Hase: 40

2. Hotel Residenz Passau: 40

1. Hotel David: 40

2. Hotel Bischofshof am Dom: 40

1. Dormero Hotel Kelheim: 40

2. Hotel Roter Hahn: 40

1. NH Ingolstadt: 41

2. Hotel im GVZ Ingolstadt: 41

1. Hotel Adler: 41

2. Hotel garni Fuchs: 41

6. Straubing, Germany: 41

7. Deggendorf, Germany: 42

8. Schlogen, Austria: 42

9. Linz, Austria: 42

10. Grein, Austria: 42

11. Melk, Austria: 43

12. Dürnstein, Austria: 43

13. Krems, Austria 43

1. Steigenberger Hotel and Spa: 43

2. Hotel Klinglhuber: 43

Useful Mobile Navigation Apps 45

1. Komoot: 45

2. Strava: 45

3. Google Maps: 45

4. Runtastic Road Bike GPS Cycling App: 46

5. OsmAnd: 46

Local Tourist Information Centers 47

1. Passau, Germany: 47

2. Regensburg, Germany: 47

3. Linz, Austria: 47

4. Vienna, Austria: 47

5. Bratislava, Slovakia: 48

6. Budapest, Hungary: 48

Welcome to the Donau Radweg Experience

Immerse yourself in a journey through cultural richness along the Donau Radweg. While Paris may steal the French spotlight, the trail along the Danube River unveils a tapestry of historical gems. Explore captivating cities like Regensburg, Linz, and Vienna, each bearing witness to a unique cultural legacy. As a historical crossroads and a cradle of artistic expression, this route boasts an array of masterpieces that have left an enduring mark on the human narrative.

Regensburg: The Riverside Heritage

Regensburg, nestled along the banks of the Danube, invites you to discover its medieval charm and architectural wonders. The Stone Bridge, Regensburg Cathedral, and the historic Old Town showcase a cultural panorama reflecting centuries of influence.

Linz: Where Innovation Meets Tradition

Linz seamlessly blends innovation and tradition, offering a glimpse into Austria's cultural evolution. Explore the Ars Electronica Center, delve into the rich musical heritage at the Brucknerhaus, and meander through the charming streets of the Old Town.

Vienna: Symphony of Imperial Splendor

Vienna resonates with echoes of Mozart, Beethoven, and Strauss as it stands as an imperial city. Immerse yourself in opulence at Schönbrunn Palace or marvel at St. Stephen's Cathedral while experiencing cultural resonance at Belvedere Palace.

The Donau Radweg is not just about cities; it unveils hidden cultural gems. From Melk Abbey's ancient allure to Wachau Valley's charming vineyards and Dürnstein's medieval mystique - this trail promises cultural exploration beyond what is expected.

Scenic Serenity

Step into a world where nature and adventure harmonize along the Donau Radweg. The landscapes unfold before you offering diverse experiences from majestic Alps in west to tranquil plains in Hungary in east. The meandering path of Danube River becomes your guide through picturesque scenes and outdoor escapades.

Alpine Majesty

Encounter the majestic beauty of the Alps as you ride through scenic paths, with snow-capped peaks and pristine lakes creating a breathtaking backdrop. Whether you're cycling through the Austrian Alps or exploring charming Bavarian villages, the Donau Radweg offers a symphony of natural wonders.

Navigate through the twists and turns of the Danube River, discovering enchanting landscapes such as vineyard-clad hills of Wachau or serene meadows along Danube Bend. Engage in water activities, from kayaking through Schlögener Schlinge to exploring hidden river islands.

Culinary Cruising

Indulge in a culinary journey along the Donau Radweg, where each stop unveils a palette of local flavors and gastronomic delights. From hearty Bavarian dishes in Passau to aromatic wines of Wachau Valley, savor the diverse tastes of regions along Danube.

Passau: Bavarian Gastronomic Haven

Explore culinary treasures at Passau where traditional Bavarian cuisine meets innovative culinary creations. Enjoy a riverside feast with local specialties complemented by historic charm of Old Town.

Wachau Valley: Vineyard Elegance

Pedal through Wachau Valley - haven for wine enthusiasts. Tantalize your taste buds with exquisite local wines paired with stunning backdrop of vineyards and medieval castles.

Diverse and Delicious

From hearty goulash in Budapest to delectable pastries in Bratislava, culinary offerings along Donau Radweg promise delightful journey for your taste buds.

Whether you're captivated by cultural wonders, enchanted by scenic landscapes or indulging in diverse flavors of region - Donau Radweg beckons with an unforgettable travel experience.

1. Passau, Germany:

Passau, a city with a fascinating history, serves as a meeting point for different cultures. It has seen the influence of ancient Roman civilization and thrived as a bustling trading center during medieval times. One of the main attractions in Passau is St. Stephen's Cathedral, which boasts the distinction of having the largest cathedral organ in the world. To fully enjoy your visit to Passau, it is recommended to plan your trip between late spring and early autumn when the weather is pleasant. The cathedral generally welcomes visitors from 6:30 AM to 6:30 PM. For more information and inquiries, you can contact Passau Tourism at +49 851 393-0 or visit their website at [Passau Tourism](https://www.passau.de/).

Regensburg, a UNESCO World Heritage Site, boasts a rich history that traces back to the Roman times. Its medieval architecture stands as a testament to its historical importance. One of its key attractions is the Stone Bridge, an architectural marvel dating back to the 12th century. If you're planning a visit, the best time to go is from May to September when the weather is warmest. The Stone Bridge is accessible at all hours, allowing visitors to admire its beauty at their convenience. For more information and inquiries, you can contact Regensburg Tourism at +49 941 507-4410 or visit their website [here](https://tourismus.regensburg.de/).

Kelheim holds a rich history in Bavaria, and Weltenburg Abbey, established in 620, stands as one of the oldest monasteries in the region. It is known for its remarkable beer and stunning baroque architecture. For the most pleasant weather, it is recommended to visit between April and October. Weltenburg Abbey welcomes visitors every day; you can find specific opening hours on their official website. If you need to get in touch with them, you can contact them at +49 9441 2008-0.

4. Ingolstadt, Germany:

When exploring the history of Ingolstadt, it's fascinating to learn about its medieval fortifications and the significant role they played in the Bavarian War of Succession. One key attraction that shouldn't be missed is the Bavarian Army Museum, which houses an extensive collection of military artifacts. If you're planning a visit, it's best to go between June and August when temperatures are warm and pleasant. To get accurate information about opening hours, be sure to check the official website of the Bavarian Army Museum. If you have any inquiries or need assistance, feel free to reach out at +49 841 937 08-0.

5. Eichstätt, Germany:

Eichstätt Cathedral, dating back to the 8th century, holds great significance as a testament to the city's rich religious heritage. This historical landmark, along with the splendid Bishop's Residence in the baroque style, is a major attraction for visitors. If you're planning a trip, it's best to visit between May and September when the weather is delightful. The cathedral typically welcomes visitors from 7:00 AM to 7:00 PM. For more information and inquiries, you can contact Eichstätt Tourism at +49 8421 50-0 or visit their website [here](https://www.tourismus-eichstaett.de/).

Straubing's Gäuboden Museum is a fascinating place that displays the rich cultural and historical journey of the city. It beautifully captures the evolution of Straubing over time. When you visit, make sure to explore not only the museum but also take a stroll along the picturesque Danube waterfront, which is another major highlight of this charming city.

To fully enjoy your visit, it is recommended to plan your trip between April and October when you can indulge in various outdoor activities. The pleasant weather during these months adds an extra charm to your experience.

If you want to know more about the opening hours of Gäuboden Museum, it's best to check their official website for accurate details. The timings may vary depending on different occasions and seasons, so it's always good to stay updated.

For any further inquiries or assistance, feel free to contact Gäuboden Museum at +49 9421 944-551. Their friendly staff will be more than happy to help you with any information or questions you may have about your visit.

Have a wonderful time exploring Straubing and immersing yourself in its rich history and vibrant culture at Gäuboden Museum!

7. Deggendorf, Germany:

Deggendorf, with its rich history, showcases a remarkable blend of medieval architecture. The town's historic buildings are a testament to its roots from that era. One of the key attractions in Deggendorf is the Lower Bavarian Railway Museum. This museum offers visitors a unique glimpse into the world of railways and their significance in the region. To make the most of your visit, it is recommended to plan your trip between May and September when the weather is pleasant and mild. The Lower Bavarian Railway Museum has specified opening hours, which can be found on their official website for more details. If you need any further information or have any inquiries, you can contact them at +49 991 3811-106.

8. Schlogen, Austria:

The Schlögener Schlinge has been a natural wonder along the Danube for centuries, with its rich history and unique meander in the river. If you're planning a visit, the best time to go is between May and September, as you'll get the best views of this breathtaking sight. Unfortunately, there is no specific contact information available for further inquiries.

Linz, a city known for its modernity, holds a fascinating cultural heritage that stretches back to the days of ancient Rome. One of its prominent highlights is the Ars Electronica Center, a vibrant hub where contemporary arts and technology converge. If you're planning a visit, it's best to schedule it between April and October when the city hosts numerous cultural events. To find out the exact opening hours of the Ars Electronica Center, you can refer to their official website. For any inquiries or assistance, feel free to reach out to them at +43 732 7272-0.

When it comes to the history of the city, Greinburg Castle stands as a remarkable testament to its medieval past. This majestic castle was constructed in the 15th century, serving as a living reminder of times long gone.

One of the key attractions in Grein is undoubtedly Greinburg Castle, with its captivating presence and rich historical significance. Alongside this magnificent structure, visitors can also explore the charming Grein Old Town, adding to the allure of this place.

To make the most out of your visit, it is recommended to plan your trip between May and October when the weather is pleasant and conducive for exploration. This allows you to fully immerse yourself in all that Grein has to offer.

For specific details regarding opening hours and schedules at Greinburg Castle, you can refer to their official website for accurate information. They provide comprehensive timing information so that you can plan your visit accordingly (website: [official website](https://www.schloss-greinburg.at/)).

If you have any inquiries or require further assistance, feel free to contact them directly at +43 7268 82440. Their friendly staff will be more than happy to assist you with any queries or concerns you may have.

11. Melk, Austria:

When it comes to the history of Melk Abbey, we can see a beautiful blend of medieval and baroque architecture. This unique combination is what makes it truly special. One of the key attractions of Melk Abbey is its stunning library, which has been recognized as a UNESCO World Heritage Site.

For those planning a visit, the best time to go is between April and October when the gardens are in full bloom. During this time, you can witness the beauty of nature surrounding the abbey.

As for opening hours, Melk Abbey is generally open from 9:00 AM to 5:30 PM. It's always good to check their website or give them a call at +43 2752 555 230 for any specific information or updates.

Visiting Melk Abbey is truly an experience like no other. The rich history and architectural wonders will leave you in awe. So make sure to add this gem to your travel itinerary!

Dürnstein Castle ruins hold captivating stories from medieval times, including the famous imprisonment of Richard the Lionheart. The castle's remnants, combined with the charming medieval streets, make for a key attraction in this historical location. For those planning a visit, it is recommended to come between May and September when the weather is pleasant. You can explore Dürnstein Castle at any time as it remains accessible throughout the day. Unfortunately, there is no specific contact information available for further inquiries.

13. Krems, Austria:

Krems, a city with a long history dating back to the Roman Empire, serves as an entrance to the rich cultural heritage of the Wachau Valley. One of its main highlights is the charming Old Town and the fascinating Krems Art Mile. If you're planning a visit, it's best to go between May and October when there are plenty of outdoor events happening. For detailed information about the opening hours of Krems Art Mile, you can check their official website at https://www.kunstmeile.at/. If you have any inquiries or need further assistance, feel free to reach out at +43 2732 82676.

Vienna, the magnificent capital of the Habsburg Empire, holds a wealth of imperial history and cultural heritage. It is a city that captivates with its grandeur and charm.

When exploring Vienna, there are several key attractions that shouldn't be missed. The Schönbrunn Palace, St. Stephen's Cathedral, and the Belvedere Palace are among the must-see landmarks that showcase the city's rich history.

Visiting Vienna can be enjoyed year-round, with the added delight of vibrant Christmas markets in December. These markets bring an extra dose of magic to the already enchanting atmosphere of the city.

The opening hours for each attraction may vary, so it's advisable to check their individual websites for specific details. This way, you can plan your visit accordingly and make the most out of your time in Vienna.

If you have any inquiries or need further information, you can contact +43 1 24 555. They will be able to assist you with any queries or concerns you may have.

Vienna truly offers a captivating experience for history enthusiasts and culture lovers alike. Its timeless beauty is something that should not be missed when embarking on a journey through Europe.

15. Bratislava, Slovakia:

Bratislava, the capital of Slovakia, has a rich history that is deeply connected to diverse European cultures. One of its main highlights is the magnificent Bratislava Castle, which stands proudly alongside the charming Old Town. If you're planning a visit, it's best to come between April and October when you can fully enjoy outdoor exploration. To find out the exact opening hours of Bratislava Castle, you can refer to their official website at https://www.bratislava.sk/. If you have any inquiries or need further information, feel free to contact them at +421 2 5935 7111.

The Gabcikovo-Nagymaros Waterworks and Dam hold a remarkable place in history as a major engineering project along the Danube. Its key attraction lies in the Gabcikovo Dam and the impressive water management system it boasts. For those planning a visit, it is recommended to go between May and September to witness the optimal water flow. As for the opening hours, specific details can be obtained on-site. Unfortunately, there is no contact information available at this time.

17. Komárno, Slovakia:

The history of Komárno's fortifications holds great significance in the annals of Central European history. These fortifications have played a crucial strategic role throughout the years, shaping the course of events in the region. One cannot miss the awe-inspiring Komárno Fortress, which stands as a testament to the city's rich heritage and architectural prowess. If you're planning a visit, it is best to go between June and August when the weather is warm and pleasant. To find out more about the opening hours of Komárno Fortress, you can check their official website for detailed timings. For any further information or inquiries, you can contact them at +421 35 694 1611.

18. Budapest, Hungary:

Budapest, situated on the banks of the Danube, boasts a rich history that traces back to its Roman roots. It is an amalgamation of two distinct parts, Buda and Pest. When exploring this captivating city, there are several key attractions that should not be missed. These include the magnificent Buda Castle, the iconic Hungarian Parliament building, and the rejuvenating Széchenyi Thermal Bath.

To make the most of your visit, it is advisable to plan your trip during spring or fall when temperatures are more moderate. The opening hours of these attractions may vary, so it is recommended to check their respective websites for accurate information.

If you have any inquiries or need further assistance, you can reach out to +36 1 438 8080 for support. Budapest offers a plethora of historical and cultural wonders waiting to be discovered!

19. Danube Bend, Hungary:

The Danube Bend holds a rich history, serving as an important intersection of both strategic and cultural significance for countless centuries. If we were to delve into its allure, we would find key attractions such as the magnificent Esztergom Basilica, the majestic Visegrád Castle, and the delightful town of

Szentendre. To make the most of your visit, it is advisable to plan it between May and October when the weather is at its finest. Keep in mind that each attraction has different opening hours, so it's best to check their respective websites for accurate information. As for contacting them, the methods may vary depending on which attraction you're interested in exploring.

Currency:
- When you embark on the Donau Radweg, the currency you'll encounter will vary depending on the country you're in. In Germany and Austria, the Euro (€) is used, while Hungary uses Hungarian Forint (HUF), and Slovakia uses Slovak Koruna (SKK). Rest assured, there are ATMs available along the way for easy currency exchange, ensuring seamless transactions during your journey.

Language:
- As you traverse the Donau Radweg, expect to come across different languages. The primary ones spoken include German, Hungarian, Slovak, and occasionally Croatian. While English is generally understood in tourist areas, it can greatly enhance your interactions with locals if you have some basic phrases in the local languages up your sleeve.

Mobile Phones:
- European mobile phones typically work well along the Donau Radweg. However, if you're traveling from other regions, make sure to check your roaming settings beforehand. To make local calls more cost-effective, consider purchasing a local SIM card.

Time:
- Since the Donau Radweg spans multiple countries, each operates according to its respective time zone. Keep this in mind when planning activities and coordinating travel arrangements to avoid any confusion caused by time differences.

Emergency Numbers:
- It's essential to familiarize yourself with vital emergency contact numbers:
  - Ambulance: Varies by country
  - Police: Varies by country
  - Fire: Varies by country
- If you need to make an emergency call from outside of a particular country, remember to use the appropriate international access code.

Useful Websites:

- Make good use of online resources for your Donau Radweg journey:

- Donau Radweg Official Site: (www.danube-cycle-path.com) - Here you'll find comprehensive information about the cycling route.

- European Railways: (www.eurail.com) - A valuable resource for train travel planning.

- Local Tourism Websites: Explore specific regions along the route to gain local insights and recommendations.

Daily Costs:

- Tailor your budget based on your preferences:

- Budget (Less than €50): Opt for affordable hostel accommodations and enjoy economical local dining options.

- Midrange (€50–€150): Indulge in comfortable hotels and explore diverse dining options along the way.

- Top End (More than €150): Treat yourself to luxury hotels, savor gourmet dining experiences, and engage in premium activities.

Opening Hours:

- Opening hours may vary along the Donau Radweg, but here are some general guidelines:

- Banks: Typically open from 9 am to 5 pm, Monday to Friday.

- Restaurants: Opening hours can vary, but you can generally expect them to be open for lunch and dinner.

- Shops: Most shops operate from 9 am to 6 pm, Monday to Saturday.

Danube Cycling Odyssey - 2 Weeks

Classic Danube Exploration
Embark on an exciting cycling adventure along the breathtaking Danube Radweg, immersing yourself in the enchanting charm of Central Europe.
Days 1 - 3: Passau, Germany
Begin your journey in the captivating city of Passau, where the Danube, Inn, and Ilz rivers converge. Take your time to explore the rich history of the Old Town, visit St. Stephen's Cathedral, and experience a unique blend of Bavarian and Austrian influences.
Days 4 - 6: Regensburg, Germany
Pedal through picturesque landscapes to reach Regensburg, a beautifully preserved medieval gem. Marvel at the magnificent Stone Bridge, wander through charming streets filled with history, and dive into the city's fascinating past.
Days 7 - 9: Linz, Austria
Cycle into Austria and arrive in Linz, a city that artfully merges modernity with tradition. Discover cultural gems like the Ars Electronica Center and immerse yourself in the vibrant atmosphere of this gem on the banks of the Danube.
Days 10 - 12: Wachau Valley, Austria
Venture into the renowned Wachau Valley known for its stunning vineyards and charming villages. Pedal through Dürnstein, Krems, and other picturesque spots while savoring every moment amidst the beauty of Austrian countryside.
Days 13 - 15: Vienna, Austria
Conclude your thrilling cycling adventure in Vienna, the imperial city along the majestic river, Danube. Explore Schönbrunn Palace, marvel at its grandeur, admire architectural marvels throughout the city, and fully indulge yourself in Vienna's rich cultural tapestry.
Historical Treasures and Natural Beauty

Days 1 - 3: Passau, Germany
Commence your exploration of the Danube Radweg in the captivating city of Passau, known as the City of Three Rivers. Uncover its medieval charm, immerse yourself in the unique Bavarian atmosphere, and get lost in its fascinating history.
Days 4 - 6: Regensburg, Germany
Pedal your way to Regensburg, a UNESCO World Heritage Site that will transport you back to medieval times. Explore its Gothic architecture, marvel at its well-preserved heritage, and appreciate every intricate detail that tells a story.
Days 7 - 9: Schlögener Schlinge, Austria
Cycle towards Schlögener Schlinge, a breathtaking meander in the Danube. Embrace the awe-inspiring natural beauty that surrounds you and let yourself be captivated by the stunning views of the Austrian landscape.
Days 10 - 12: Linz, Austria
Continue your journey to Linz, where history gracefully blends with modernity. Discover its cultural offerings, witness how contemporary life merges with the Danube's essence, and immerse yourself in this vibrant city.
Days 13 - 15: Wachau Valley, Austria
Pedal through the enchanting Wachau Valley, renowned for its vineyards and castles. Experience a harmonious blend of history and nature as you explore this captivating region filled with stories waiting to be discovered.

Danube Delta Discovery

Days 1 - 3: Passau, Germany
Embark on your cycling adventure in Passau, where the magnificent journey along the Danube begins. Uncover historical landmarks within this charming city while soaking up vibrant riverbank atmosphere that will leave a lasting impression.
Days 4 - 6: Linz, Austria
Cycle towards Linz, a city bursting with a rich cultural scene. Immerse yourself in its artistic offerings, experience the dynamic energy that fills the air, and let yourself be captivated by this gem of Austria.

Days 7 - 9: Danube Bend, Hungary

Head towards the captivating Danube Bend, a region known for its scenic beauty and historical significance. Visit Esztergom, Visegrád, and Szentendre to uncover the cultural richness that Hungary has to offer.

Days 10 - 12: Bratislava, Slovakia

Cross the border into Slovakia and explore the charming city of Bratislava. Wander through its well-preserved Old Town, visit Bratislava Castle, and immerse yourself in the captivating history that surrounds you.

Days 13 - 15: Budapest, Hungary

Conclude your epic Danube Delta journey in Budapest, the vibrant capital of Hungary. Explore Buda Castle, indulge in relaxing thermal baths, and savor every moment as you immerse yourself in the cultural and culinary delights that this magnificent city has to offer.

Embark on these diverse Danube Radweg itineraries, where you'll cycle through historic cities, picturesque landscapes, and discover hidden cultural treasures along your journey. Allow the Danube to guide you on an unforgettable adventure across Central Europe!

Welcome to the Danube Cycling Retreat - Accommodation Guide! Whether you're a seasoned traveler or an adventure seeker, there are various accommodations along the Danube Radweg that cater to every type of traveler. Let's explore the options!

1. Riverfront Inns and Guesthouses:

Indulge in scenic views and cozy comfort at charming inns and guesthouses nestled along the picturesque route of the Danube. Prices range from €60 to €120 per night, and you can opt for riverfront rooms to fully immerse yourself in the tranquil atmosphere.

2. Traditional Austrian Mountain Huts:

Experience the authentic alpine ambiance of Austrian mountain huts from June to September. These unique lodgings offer dormitory-style lodging with prices ranging from €25 to €40 per person, including breakfast. It's a great opportunity to connect with fellow travelers while enjoying the beautiful mountains.

3. Urban Retreats in Linz:

When you reach Linz, treat yourself to modern comfort blended with cultural vibes at urban retreats. From stylish hotels to boutique accommodations, prices range from €80 to €150 per night. Immerse yourself in the city's artistic scene and contemporary lifestyle.

4. Quaint B&Bs in Wachau Valley:

For a charming experience surrounded by vineyards, choose quaint bed and breakfasts in the enchanting Wachau Valley. Prices range from €50 to €90 per night, offering personalized service and warm hospitality. Wake up each morning to freshly brewed coffee and breathtaking vineyard landscapes.

5. Danube Delta Riverside Cabins:

Escape into nature by staying in riverside cabins within the unique ecosystem of the Danube Delta. Prices range from €70 to €120 per night, allowing you to immerse yourself fully in this serene environment while enjoying birdwatching and experiencing delta life.

6. Historic Pensions in Bratislava:
In Bratislava, embrace the old-world charm and central locations of historic pensions. Experience the city's rich history with prices ranging from €70 to €130 per night. Take leisurely strolls through charming streets and indulge in local cuisine at nearby cafes.
7. Budapest Boutique Hotels:
End your journey in Budapest with a touch of cultural elegance and city luxury at boutique hotels. Prices range from €100 to €200 per night, offering spa amenities, proximity to landmarks, and a vibrant atmosphere that captures the essence of the Hungarian capital.
8. Cyclist-Friendly Hostels:
Traveling on a budget? Connect with fellow cyclists at cyclist-friendly hostels along the Danube Radweg. Prices range from €20 to €40 per night, providing an affordable stay while enjoying the camaraderie of the cycling community.
9. Lakeside Campgrounds near Linz:
For nature lovers, experience lakeside camping near Linz for a refreshing retreat amidst natural beauty. Prices range from €15 to €30 per night, allowing you to enjoy camping simplicity while still being close to Linz's cultural attractions.
10. Quirky Convents along the Danube:
Discover a unique experience by staying in quirky convents along the Danube. Some prioritize spiritual retreats, while others offer reasonable prices ranging from €40 to €80 per night for travelers seeking tranquility and cultural insight.
So there you have it - a diverse range of accommodations along the Danube Radweg that cater to every traveler's preferences! Enjoy your journey and make unforgettable memories along this beautiful cycling route.

Embarking on the journey along the Danube Radweg requires a deep understanding of visa and residency regulations. Let me provide you with an informative guide to ensure a smooth and compliant travel experience:

1. Schengen Treaty for European Cyclists:

  - European cyclists hailing from countries within the Schengen Treaty can easily pedal through the Danube Radweg using a valid identity card or passport.

2. Visa Exemptions for Select Countries:

  - Cyclists from various non-EU countries, including Australia, Brazil, Canada, Israel, Japan, New Zealand, and the USA, have the privilege of visa exemptions for tourist visits lasting up to 90 days. It's essential to check specific requirements, particularly if there are plans to cross into the UK or Ireland.

3. Visas for Extended Stays and Non-Schengen Nationals:

  - For cyclists planning stays exceeding 90 days or for purposes beyond tourism (such as work or study), specific visas are necessary.

  - You can find detailed visa requirements on the official website www.embassy.gov.it or by reaching out to Italian consulates along your route.

4. Residence and Work for EU Cyclists:

  - EU cyclists have the freedom to pedal through Italy without permits initially. However, after three months of continuous residence, it becomes mandatory to register at the municipal registry office. Proof of employment or adequate financial means may be required.

5. Permanent Residence for Non-EU Adventurers:

  - Non-EU cyclists who have resided legally along the Danube route without interruption for five years can apply for permanent residence status.

6. Permit to Stay ('Permesso di Soggiorno'):

- Non-EU cyclists planning extended stays at one location exceeding a week should obtain a 'permesso di soggiorno' from the local police station.

- Tourists staying in hotels are generally exempt from this requirement.

- Obtaining a 'permesso di soggiorno' becomes crucial for cyclists engaged in study, work, or prolonged residence. The application process, which is detailed on www.poliziadistato.it, involves specific documents and may vary based on individual circumstances. EU cyclists, however, are exempt.

7. Study Visas for Cycling Scholars:

- Non-EU cyclists who intend to pursue studies at universities or language schools along the route must secure a study visa from the nearest Italian embassy or consulate.

- Required documentation usually includes proof of enrollment, fee payments, and sufficient funds to support the duration of studies.

- Study visas align with the enrollment period and can be renewed within Italy based on ongoing enrollment and financial capacity.

It's crucial for cyclists navigating the Danube Radweg to understand these visa and residency intricacies. Always cross-check with official sources to stay updated on the latest requirements, ensuring a seamless and legally compliant cycling adventure through the heart of Europe.

Embarking on the Danube Radweg is a truly mesmerizing experience, as each season brings its own unique charm and beauty to the cycling route. Let's explore the highlights of each season that will make your journey even more memorable:

Spring (March to May):

- Blooming Landscapes: Prepare to be amazed as the Danube valley awakens with a kaleidoscope of vibrant blooms. The arrival of spring showers brings an explosion of colors, turning the scenery into a picturesque wonderland.

- Mild Temperatures: Enjoy delightful weather for cycling, with mild temperatures that make it perfect for pedaling through charming towns and countryside.

Summer (June to August):

- Festivals and Events: Immerse yourself in the lively atmosphere of summer festivals held in towns along the route. Experience cultural celebrations and local music events that showcase the vibrant traditions of the Danube.

- River Cruises: Witness elegant cruise ships gracefully navigating through the waterways during summer. Share the scenic beauty of the Danube with these majestic vessels, adding an extra touch of dynamism.

Autumn (September to November):

- Foliage and Harvest: Pedal through a breathtaking palette of autumnal colors as you cycle along riverbanks. Experience nature's artwork as vineyards in Wachau and other regions come alive with stunning shades of red, orange, and gold.

- Wine Tours: Autumn is harvest season, making it an excellent time for wine enthusiasts to indulge in their passion. Join local wine tours and savor the rich flavors offered by the Danube's renowned wine-producing regions.

Winter (December to February):

- Snowy Landscapes: Encounter a serene side of the Danube as winter blankets this region in pristine white snow. While cycling may be limited, take the opportunity to appreciate the peacefulness of the riverside adorned in a snowy veil.

- Christmas Markets: Delight in the enchanting Christmas markets that come alive in towns along the route. Immerse yourself in festive decorations, indulge in seasonal treats, and embrace the warm holiday spirit amidst a cozy winter setting.

Year-Round Attractions:

- Historic Castles and Monasteries: Be captivated by the timeless beauty of castles and monasteries that grace this landscape. Whether wrapped in a snowy embrace during winter or surrounded by lush greenery in summer, these landmarks never fail to inspire awe.

- Culinary Delights: Indulge your taste buds with local culinary delights that can be enjoyed throughout the year. From hearty winter stews to fresh summer produce, the Danube offers a feast for your senses with its diverse culinary offerings.

No matter which season you choose, the Danube Radweg promises an enchanting tale waiting to unfold. Plan your journey around these seasonal highlights that resonate with your interests, and create memories that will span across every facet of the ever-changing charm of the Danube.

Embarking on the Donau Radweg unveils an exhilarating cycling adventure along the enchanting Danube River. Let's delve into this picturesque route, breaking it down into manageable sections, and providing you with insights into key landmarks, charming towns, and breathtaking scenic spots.

1. Passau, Germany, to Regensburg, Germany:
   - Distance: Covering approximately 127 km
   - Highlights:
     - Begin your journey in Passau where the Danube, Inn, and Ilz rivers converge.
     - Immerse yourself in the Bavarian countryside as you cycle through quaint villages and lush landscapes.
     - Arrive at Regensburg, a UNESCO World Heritage Site renowned for its medieval charm and the iconic Stone Bridge.

2. Regensburg, Germany to Kelheim, Germany:
   - Distance: Spanning around 45 km
   - Highlights:
     - Explore Regensburg's Old Town and its historic landmarks.
     - Pedal through scenic paths that lead you to Kelheim.
     - Discover the Weltenburg Abbey and embark on a boat trip through the Danube Gorge for awe-inspiring scenery.

3. Kelheim, Germany to Ingolstadt, Germany:
   - Distance: Covering approximately 67 km
   - Highlights:
     - Traverse through the splendid Danube Valley surrounded by vineyards and rolling hills.
     - Immerse yourself in Ingolstadt's rich history encompassing medieval fortifications and the Bavarian Army Museum.

4. Ingolstadt, Germany to Eichstätt, Germany:
   - Distance: Spanning around 55 km
   - Highlights:
     - Pedal through charming Bavarian landscapes adorned with picturesque villages.

- Explore Eichstätt, home to the magnificent Eichstätt Cathedral and the Bishop's Residence, a baroque masterpiece.

5. Eichstätt, Germany to Straubing, Germany:

   - Distance: Covering approximately 100 km

   - Highlights:

   - Ride through the scenic Altmühltal Nature Park and soak in its natural beauty.

   - Immerse yourself in the rich Bavarian culture of Straubing while exploring attractions like the Gäuboden Museum and Danube waterfront.

6. Straubing, Germany to Deggendorf, Germany:

   - Distance: Spanning around 54 km

   - Highlights:

   - Revel in the mesmerizing beauty of the Danube as it gracefully winds its way through Bavaria.

   - Pay a visit to Deggendorf and appreciate its historic architecture while exploring local museums.

7. Deggendorf, Germany to Schlogen, Austria:

   - Distance: Covering approximately 83 km

   - Highlights:

   - Admire the picturesque landscapes that unfold along the Danube as you pedal forward.

   - Reach Schlogen and marvel at the Schlögener Schlinge, a spectacular meander in the river.

8. Schlogen, Austria to Linz, Austria:

   - Distance: Spanning around 60 km

   -Highlights:

   - Cycle through idyllic Austrian countryside adorned with charming villages.

   - Uncover Linz's blend of modernity and tradition as you explore cultural institutions like the Ars Electronica Center.

9. Linz, Austria, to Grein, Austria:

   - Distance: Covering approximately 60 km

   - Highlights:

   - Immerse yourself in the breathtaking beauty of the Danube as you pedal along.

- Discover the historical wonders of Greinburg Castle, which happens to be Austria's oldest residential castle. And don't forget to explore Grein's charming Old Town.

10. Grein, Austria, to Melk, Austria:
  - Distance: Spanning around 60 km
  - Highlights:
  - Cycle through the picturesque Wachau Valley with its lush vineyards and quaint towns.
  - Make a stop at Melk Abbey—a majestic Benedictine monastery perched atop a hill and offering panoramic views of the Danube.

11. Melk, Austria, to Dürnstein, Austria:
  - Distance: Covering approximately 40 km
  - Highlights:
  - Lose yourself in the medieval charm of Dürnstein as you wander through its narrow streets.
  - For an awe-inspiring experience, hike up to Dürnstein Castle ruins and be rewarded with breathtaking vistas of the Danube.

12. Dürnstein, Austria, to Krems,Austria:
  - Distance: Stretching around 35 km
  - Highlights:
  - Immerse yourself in Krems' vibrant culture—famous for its wine production,
    artistic heritage,and architectural marvels.
  - Stroll along its charming streets and treat your taste buds to local culinary delights.

13. Krems,Austria, to Vienna, Austria:
  - Distance: Covering approximately 80 km
  - Highlights:
  - Traverse the enchanting Danube Bend, where rolling hills and charming towns paint a picturesque backdrop.
  - Conclude your journey in Vienna—the city of imperial palaces, world-class museums, and the iconic St. Stephen's Cathedral.

Key Junctions on the Donau Radweg

Let's embark on a journey along the Donau Radweg, exploring key junctions that offer unique experiences and breathtaking sights.
1. Passau, Germany - The Gateway to Cycling Adventure:
  - Our adventure begins in Passau, where the Danube, Inn, and Ilz rivers come together.
  - Highlights: Marvel at the Passau Cathedral, explore Veste Oberhaus, and wander through the charming Old Town.
2. Regensburg, Germany - A Glimpse of Medieval Majesty:
  - Immerse yourself in Regensburg's well-preserved medieval charm in the heart of its Old Town.
  - Highlights: Cross the historic Stone Bridge, admire Regensburg Cathedral's grandeur, and savor a meal at the Historic Sausage Kitchen.
3. Kelheim, Germany - Gateway to Breathtaking Scenery:
  - Discover the awe-inspiring Weltenburg Abbey and embark on a boat trip through the scenic Danube Gorge.
  - Highlights: Experience the natural beauty of Danube Gorge, visit Liberation Hall (Befreiungshalle), and explore Befreiungshalle Kelheim.
4. Ingolstadt, Germany - Dive into History:
  - Immerse yourself in Ingolstadt's rich history as you explore medieval fortifications and delve into Bavarian military heritage at Bavarian Army Museum.
  - Highlights: Marvel at Ingolstadt Fortress (Ingolstädter Veste), admire Asam Church's architectural beauty, and delve into Bavarian Army Museum.
5. Eichstätt, Germany - A Treat for Baroque Enthusiasts:
  - Admire Baroque architecture at its finest with visits to Eichstätt Cathedral and Bishop's Residence.
  - Highlights: Explore Willibaldsburg Castle perched atop a hill, soak in nature's beauty at Altmühltal Nature Park, and stroll through the Baroque Residence Square.
6. Straubing, Germany - Bavarian Cultural Gem:

- Immerse yourself in the rich Bavarian culture as you explore Gäuboden Museum and enjoy a leisurely stroll along the Danube waterfront.

 - Highlights: Discover the treasures of Gäubodenmuseum, marvel at Herzogsschloss Straubing's grandeur, and embark on a delightful Danube Cruise.

7. Deggendorf, Germany - Haven of Historic Architecture:

 - Admire the architectural wonders of Deggendorf and delve into local history at Lower Bavarian Railway Museum.

 - Highlights: Visit St. Peter and Paul's Church, explore Deggendorf Town Square, and appreciate art at Danube Art Museum.

8. Schlogen, Austria - Unleash the Beauty of Nature:

 - Marvel at the unique natural beauty of Schlögener Schlinge, a mesmerizing meander in the Danube.

 - Highlights: Take in breathtaking views from Schlögener Schlinge Viewpoint, visit Donaublick Observation Platform, and explore Engelhartszell Abbey.

9. Linz, Austria - Where Modernity Meets Tradition:

 - Experience the perfect blend of modernity and tradition in Linz.

 - Highlights: Explore futuristic exhibits at Ars Electronica Center, admire Linz Castle's architectural splendor,

   and discover art masterpieces at Lentos Art Museum.

10. Grein, Austria – Castle Charm and Old Town Delights:

 – Step into history as you explore Greinburg Castle—the oldest residential castle in Austria.

 – Key Highlights: Roam around Greinburg Castle's magnificent halls,

   enjoy a performance at Grein Historic Theater,

   or simply soak up the atmosphere in charming Grein Old Town.

11. Melk Abbey – A Monastic Marvel:

 – Marvel at the grandeur of Melk Abbey, a Benedictine monastery overlooking the Danube.

 – Key Highlights: Explore the beautiful Wachau Valley,

   wander through Melk Old Town's picturesque streets.

12. Dürnstein, Austria – Mystique of Medieval Times:

– Immerse yourself in the medieval ambiance as you wander through Dürnstein's narrow streets

and hike up to the ruins of Dürnstein Castle.

– Key Highlights: Discover the history behind Dürnstein Castle, admire the iconic Blue Tower,

and visit Dürnstein Abbey.

13. Krems, Austria – Wine, Art, and Historic Charm:

– Experience the cultural richness of Krems with its renowned wine, vibrant art scene,

and well-preserved historic architecture.

– Key Highlights: Explore Krems Old Town's charming streets, pass through Steiner Tor (Stone Gate),

and visit Göttweig Abbey for a spiritual experience.

Passau, Germany offers a selection of charming hotels for travelers to choose from. Let's take a look at some of the top options:
1. Hotel Weisser Hase:
  - Located at Rindermarkt 6, 94032 Passau, Germany.
  - You can reach them at +49 851 35010.
  - For more information, visit their website: [Hotel Weisser Hase](https://www.weisser-hase.de/en/).
2. Hotel Residenz Passau:
  - Situated at Fritz-Schäffer-Promenade 6, 94032 Passau, Germany.
  - Contact them at +49 851 93110.
  - Explore their website for further details: [Hotel Residenz Passau](https://www.residenz-passau.de/en/).
If you're planning a visit to Regensburg, Germany, here are two noteworthy hotels:
1. Hotel David:
  - Found at Goldene-Bären-Straße 7, 93047 Regensburg, Germany.
  - Feel free to call them at +49 941 5993880.
  - Check out their website for more information: [Hotel David](https://www.hotel-david.de/).
2. Hotel Bischofshof am Dom:
  - Located at Krauterermarkt 3, 93047 Regensburg, Germany.
  - Reach them via telephone at +49 941 29870.
  - Visit their website to discover more: [Hotel Bischofshof am Dom](https://www.bischofshof.de/).
In Kelheim, Germany, you'll find these wonderful hotel options:
1. Dormero Hotel Kelheim:
  - Situated at Donauweg 4, 93309 Kelheim, Germany.
  - Contact them at +49 9441 18080.
  - For more details, visit their website: [Dormero Hotel Kelheim](https://www.dormero.de/en/hotel-kelheim/).
2. Hotel Roter Hahn:

- Located at Donauweg 1, 93309 Kelheim, Germany.
- Reach them via telephone at +49 9441 1750.
- Explore their website for further information: [Hotel Roter Hahn](https://www.roter-hahn-kelheim.de/).
If you're heading to Ingolstadt, Germany, consider these hotels:
1. NH Ingolstadt:
  - Found at Goethestraße 153, 85055 Ingolstadt, Germany.
  - Feel free to call them at +49 841 95140.
  - Check out their website for more information: [NH Ingolstadt](https://www.nh-hotels.com/hotel/nh-ingolstadt).
2. Hotel im GVZ Ingolstadt:
  - Located at Sophie-Scholl-Straße 14, 85055 Ingolstadt, Germany.
  - Reach them via telephone at +49 841 981120.
  - Visit their website to discover more: [Hotel im GVZ Ingolstadt](https://www.hotel-im-gvz.de/).
Lastly, in Eichstätt, Germany, you can consider these options:
1. Hotel Adler:
  - Situated at Residenzplatz 2, 85072 Eichstätt, Germany.
  - Contact them at +49 8421 90040.
  - For more details about the hotel, visit their website: [Hotel Adler](https://www.hotel-adler-eichstaett.de/).
2. Hotel garni Fuchs:
      - Located at Ostenstraße 20, 85072 Eichstätt, Germany.
  - Reach them via telephone at +49 8421 20099.
  - Explore their website for further information: [Hotel garni Fuchs](https://www.hotel-fuchs-eichstaett.de/).
6. Straubing, Germany:
  - Hotel Theresientor
    - Located at Theresienplatz 20, 94315 Straubing, Germany
    - You can reach them at +49 9421 1870
    - Check out their website: [Hotel Theresientor](https://www.hotel-theresientor.de/)
  - Hotel Gäubodenhof
    - Situated at Wittelsbacherhöhe 32, 94315 Straubing, Germany
    - Contact them at +49 9421 1860
    - Visit their website: [Hotel Gäubodenhof](https://www.hotel-gaeubodenhof.de/)

7. Deggendorf, Germany:
  - NH Deggendorf
    - Found at Edlmairstraße 4, 94469 Deggendorf, Germany
    - Call them at +49 991 34250
    - Explore their website: [NH Deggendorf](https://www.nh-hotels.com/hotel/nh-deggendorf)
  - Hotel Burgwirt
    - Located at Fischerdorf 6, 94469 Deggendorf, Germany
    - Reach out to them at +49 9912705
    – Visit their website: [Hotel Burgwirt](https://www.burgwirt.de/)
8. Schlogen, Austria:
  – Hotel Donauschlinge
  – Address is Schlögen2 ,4083 Haibach ob der Donau,Austria
  – You can call them on +43727985440
  – Find more information here :[Hotel Donauschlinge](https://www.donauschlinge.at/)
  - Pension Feiken
    - Located at Schlögen 17, 4083 Haibach ob der Donau, Austria
    - Contact them at +43 7279 8212
    - Check out their website: [Pension Feiken](https://www.feiken.at/)
9. Linz, Austria:
  - Park Inn by Radisson Linz
    – Can be found at Hessenplatz 16-18, 4020 Linz, Austria
    – Telephone: +43 73277710
    – Visit their website: [Park Inn by Radisson Linz](https://www.parkinn.com/linz)
  - Austria Trend Hotel Schillerpark Linz
    – Address is Rainerstraße 2-4 ,4020 Linz,Austria
    – You can call them on +4373269760
    – Find more information here :[Austria Trend Hotel Schillerpark Linz](https://www.austria-trend.at/en/hotels/schillerpark)
10. Grein, Austria:
  - Hotel Goldenes Kreuz:
    - Located at Stadtplatz 8, 4360 Grein, Austria.
    - Contact them at +43 7268 6103.

  - Visit their website [here](https://www.hotel-goldenes-kreuz.at/).
   - Hotel Zur Traube:
    - You can find it at Stadtplatz 76, 4360 Grein, Austria.
    - Give them a call at +43 7268 6338.
    - Check out their website [here](http://www.hotel-zur-traube.at/).
11. Melk, Austria:
   - Hotel Restaurant zur Post:
    - Address: Hauptstraße 2, 3390 Melk, Austria
    - Telephone: +43 2752 52080
    - Website: [Hotel Restaurant zur Post](https://www.hotelzurpost-melk.at/)
   - Hotel Wachau:
    - Address: Am Wachberg 3, 3390 Melk, Austria
    - Telephone: +43 2752 54065
    - Website: [Hotel Wachau](https://www.hotelwachau.at/)
12. Dürnstein, Austria:
     - Hotel Richard Löwenherz:
     - Located at Dürnstein 6,3601 Dürnstein,Austria
     - Get in touch with them by calling +43 (2711)210
     - To learn more about this hotel visit their site here:[Hotel Richard Löwenherz](https://www.loewenherz.at/)
     -Gartenhotel & Weingut Pfeffel Dürnstein:
     - Address: Dürnstein 60, 3601 Dürnstein, Austria
     - You can reach them at +43 (2711)234
     - For more information about this hotel visit their website here:[Gartenhotel & Weingut Pfeffel Dürnstein](https://www.pfeffel-duernstein.at/)
13. Krems, Austria
1. Steigenberger Hotel and Spa:
   - Located at Am Goldberg 2, 3500 Krems an der Donau, Austria.
   - You can reach them at +43 2732 71010.
   - Check out their website [here](https://www.steigenberger.com/en/hotels/all-hotels/austria/krems-an-der-donau/steigenberger-hotel-and-spa).
2. Hotel Klinglhuber:

  - Their address is Wiener Straße 10, 3500 Krems an der Donau, Austria.
  - Contact them at +43 2732 83191.
  - Visit their website [here](https://www.klinglhuber.at/).

If you're looking to make your cycling experience along the Donau Radweg smoother and more convenient, mobile navigation apps are here to help. These apps provide real-time information, route planning, and essential features that will guide you along the Danube. Here are some highly recommended mobile navigation apps that you should consider:

1. Komoot:
  - Features:
    - Enjoy turn-by-turn voice navigation.
    - Access offline maps for areas with limited connectivity.
    - Plan your route with elevation profiles in mind.
    - Discover interesting points of interest and highlights along the way.
  - Availability: You can find Komoot on both Android and iOS platforms.
  - Website: [Komoot](https://www.komoot.com/)
2. Strava:
  - Features:
    - Utilize GPS tracking to record your routes accurately.
    - Engage in friendly competition with segments and leaderboards.
    - Benefit from route planning based on popular paths.
    - Integrate Strava with your fitness tracking devices for a seamless experience.
  - Availability: Strava is available for both Android and iOS users.
  - Website: [Strava](https://www.strava.com/)
3. Google Maps:
  - Features:
    - Count on reliable navigation services from Google Maps, a widely-used platform.
    - Get cycling directions that include elevation information to better plan your journey.
    – Stay updated with real-time traffic updates along the way

– Find points of interest, restaurants, and accommodations conveniently displayed on the map

– Availability: You can access Google Maps on both Android and iOS devices

– Website:[Google Maps](https://www.google.com/maps)

4. Runtastic Road Bike GPS Cycling App:

Features:

Track your rides accurately using GPS technology

Benefit from voice coaching to improve your performance

Access offline maps for navigation without relying on data

Integrate the app with fitness sensors for a comprehensive experience

Availability: You can download Runtastic Road Bike GPS Cycling App on both Android and iOS devices.

Website: [Runtastic](https://www.runtastic.com/)

5. OsmAnd:

- Features:

- Enjoy detailed offline maps that provide comprehensive information.

- Receive turn-by-turn voice navigation instructions for a hassle-free journey.

- Explore points of interest and even integrate Wikipedia for additional insights.

- Discover dedicated cycling and hiking routes to suit your preferences.

- Availability: OsmAnd is available on both Android and iOS platforms.

- Website: [OsmAnd](https://osmand.net/)

Before embarking on your cycling adventure along the Donau Radweg, we strongly recommend downloading these apps. This way, you can have access to offline maps and test out the features beforehand, ensuring a seamless navigation experience throughout your journey.

Local Tourist Information Centers

Discovering the wonders of the Donau Radweg is made easier with the assistance of Local Tourist Information Centers. These centers play a vital role in providing valuable information, maps, and support to cyclists embarking on this adventure. Let's take a look at some key Tourist Information Centers you can find along the route:

1. Passau, Germany:
   - Address: Rathausplatz 2, 94032 Passau, Germany
   - Telephone: +49 851 398600
   - Services:
     - They offer detailed maps of the Donau Radweg.
     - You can get information on local attractions and accommodations.
     - They are ready to assist you with route planning.

2. Regensburg, Germany:
   - Address: Altes Rathaus, Rathausplatz 1, 93047 Regensburg, Germany
   - Telephone: +49 941 5074410
   - Services:
     - Get reliable Donau Radweg route information here.
     - You'll find brochures highlighting Regensburg's historic sites.
     - Accommodation recommendations are also available.

3. Linz, Austria:
   - Address: Hauptplatz 1, 4020 Linz, Austria
   - Telephone: +43 732 70700
   - Services:
     - Maps and information specific to the Donau Radweg can be obtained here.
     - They'll suggest cultural activities for you to enjoy in Linz.
     _ In case you have any queries related to your route, they will provide assistance.

4. Vienna, Austria:
   _ Address: Albertinaplatz ,1010 Vienna ,Austria
    Telephone:+43-1-24555

Services:

   Donau Radweg maps and directions are available here.

   You can also find brochures that highlight Vienna's attractions.

   General tourist information is provided as well.

5. Bratislava, Slovakia:

   - Address: Klobučnícka 2, 811 01 Bratislava, Slovakia

   - Telephone: +421 2/5443 3715

   - Services:

   - Get information about the Donau Radweg in Slovakia from this center.

   - Brochures are available to showcase Bratislava's landmarks.

   - They can assist you with cross-border travel.

6. Budapest, Hungary:

   - Address: Báthory utca 22, 1054 Budapest, Hungary

   - Telephone: +36 1 438 8080

   - Services:

   - Donau Radweg maps and cycling resources are provided here.

   - Receive recommendations for exploring Budapest from the knowledgeable staff.

   _ Stay updated on local events with their information service.

These Tourist Information Centers serve as valuable resources for cyclists, offering guidance and local insights to ensure a seamless Donau Radweg experience. It is recommended to check the opening hours and services offered by each center for the most accurate and up-to-date information.